S				
		A				
A	R	C	H	I	V	E
		R				
		E				
		D				

For access to all original manuscripts and material for Heptameron,

Visit www.sacred-archive.com/pda

Table of Contents

Heptameron:
or,
Magical Elements
of
Peter de Abano, philosopher

In the former book, which is the fourth book of *Agrippa*, it is sufficiently spoken concerning Magical Ceremonies, and Initiations.

But because he seemeth to have written to the learned, and well-experienced in this art; because he doth not specially treat of the Ceremonies, but rather speaketh of them in general, it was therefore thought good to adde hereunto the Magical Elements of *Peter de Abano* : that those who are hitherto ignorant, and have not tasted of Magical Superstitions, may have them in readiness, how they may exercise themselves therein. For we see in this book, as it were a certain introduction of Magical vanity; and, as if they were in present exercise, they may behold the distinct functions of spirits, how they may be drawn to discourse and communication; what is to be done every day, and every hour; and how they shall be read, as if they were described sillable by sillable.

In brief, in this book are kept the principles of Magical conveyances. But because the greatest power is attributed to the Circles; (For they are certain fortresses to defend the operators safe from the evil Spirits;) In the first place we will treat concerning the composition of a Circle.

Of the Circle, and the Composition Thereof.

The form of Circles is not alwaies one and the same; but useth to be changed, according to the order of the Spirits that are to be called, their places, times, daies and hours. For in making a Circle, it ought to be considered in what time of the year, what day, and what hour, that you make the Circle; what Spirits you would call, to what Star and Region they do belong, and what fuctions they have. Therefore let there be made three Circles of the latitude of nine foot, and let them be distant one from another a hands breadth; and in the middle Circle, first, write the name of the hour wherein you do the work. In the second place, Write the name of the Angel of the hour. In the third place, The Sigil of the Angel of the hour. Fourthly, The name of the Angel that ruleth that day wherein you do the work, and the names of his ministers. In the fifth place, The name of the present time. Sixthly, The name of the Spirits ruling in that part of time, and their Presidents. Seventhly, The name of the head of the Signe ruling in that part of time wherein you work. Eighthly, The name of the earth, according to that part of time wherein you work. Ninthly, and for the compleating of the middle Circle, Write the name of the Sun and of the Moon, according to the said rule of time; for as the time is changed, so the names are to be altered. And in the outermost Circle, let there be drawn in the four Angles, the names of the presidential Angels of the Air, that day wherein you would do this work; to wit, the name of the King and his three Ministers. Without the Circle, in four Angles, let *Pentagones* be made. In the inner Circle let there be written four divine names with crosses interposed in the middle of the Circle; to wit, towards the East let there be written Alpha, and towards the West let there be written *Omega*; and let a cross divide the middle of the Circle. When the Circle is thus finished, according to the rule now before written, you shall proceed.

Of the Names of the Hours, and the Angels ruling them.

It is also to be known, that the Angels do rule the hours in a successive order, according to the course of the heavens, and Planets unto which they are subject; so that that Spirit which governeth the day, ruleth also the first hour of the day; the second from this governeth the second hour; the third; the third hour, and so consequently: and when seven Planets and hours have made their revolution, it returneth again to the first which ruleth the day. Therefore we shall first speak of the names of the hours.

Hours of the day:	Hours of the night:
1. Yayn.	*1. Beron.*
2. Janor.	*2. Barol.*
3. Nasnia.	*3. Thanu.*
4. Salla.	*4. Athir.*
5. Sadedali.	*5. Mathon.*
6. Thamur.	*6. Rana.*
7. Ourer.	*7. Netos.*
8. Thamic.	*8. Tafrac.*
9. Neron.	*9. Sassur.*
10. Jayon.	*10. Aglo.*
11. Abai.	*11. Calerna.*
12. Natalon.	*12. Salam.*

Of the Names of the Hours, and the Angels ruling them.

Of the names of the Angels and their Sigils, it shall be spoken in their proper places. Now let us take a view of the names of the times. A year therefore is fourfold, and is divided into the Spring, Summer, Harvest and Winter; the names whereof are these.

The Spring.	*Talvi.*
The Summer.	*Casmaran.*
Autumne.	*Ardarael.*
Winter.	*Farlas.*

THE ANGELS OF THE SPRING.

Caratasa.	*Core.*
Amatiel.	*Commissoros.*

THE HEAD OF THE SIGNE OF SPRING.

Spugliguel.

THE NAMES OF THE EARTH IN THE SPRING.

Amadai.

THE NAMES OF THE SUN AND THE MOON IN THE SPRING.

The Sun.	The Moon.
Abraym.	*Agusita.*

Heptameron: or, Magical Elements of Peter de Abano, philosopher

THE ANGELS OF THE SUMMER.

Gargatel.

Tariel.

Gaviel.

THE HEAD OF THE SIGNE OF SUMMER.

Festativi.

THE NAMES OF THE SUN AND MOON IN SUMMER.

The Sun.	The Moon.
Athemay.	*Armatus.*

THE ANGELS OF AUTUMNE.

Tarquam.

Guabarel.

THE HEAD OF THE SIGNE OF AUTUMNE.

Tarquaret.

THE NAME OF THE EARTH IN AUTUMNE.

Rabianara.

Of the Names of the Hours, and the Angels ruling them.

THE NAMES OF THE SUN AND MOON IN AUTUMNE.

The Sun.   The Moon.

Abragini.   *Matasignais.*

THE ANGELS OF WINTER.

Amabael.

Ctarari.

THE NAME OF THE EARTH IN WINTER.

Geremiah.

THE NAMES OF THE SUN AND MOON IN WINTER.

The Sun.   The Moon.

Commutaff.   *Affaterim.*

The Consecrations and Benedictions: and first of the Benediction of the Circle.

When the Circle is ritely perfected, sprinkle the same with holy or purging water, and say, *Thou shalt purge me with hysop, (O Lord,) and I shall be clean: Thou shalt wash me, and I shall be whiter then snow.*

The Benediction of perfumes.

The God of Abraham, God of Isaac, God of Jacob, bless here the creatures of these kindes, that they may fill up the power and vertue of their odours; so that neither the enemy, nor any false imagination, may be able to enter into them: through our Lord Jesus Christ, &c. Then let them be sprinkled with holy water.

The Exorcisme of the fire upon which the perfumes are to be put.

The fire which is to be used for suffumigations, is to be in a new vessel of earth or iron; and let it be exorcised after this manner. *I exorcise thee, O thou creature of fire, by him by whom all things are made, that forthwith thou cast away every phantasme from thee, that it shall not be able to do any hurt in any thing.* Then say, *Bless, O Lord, this creature of fire, and sanctifie it, that it may be blessed to set forth the praise of thy holy name, that no hurt may come to the Exorcisers or Spectators: through our Lord Jesus Christ, &c.*

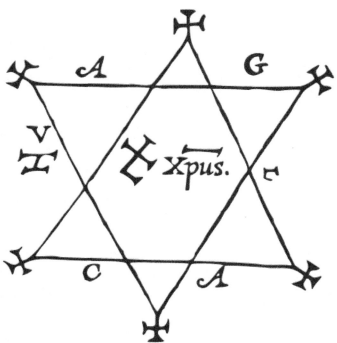

Of the Garment and Pentacle.

Let it be a Priests Garment, if it can be had, let it be of linen, and clean. Then take this Pentacle made in the day and hour of Mercury, the Moon increasing, written in parchment made of a kids skin. But first let there be said over it the Mass of the holy Ghost, and let it be sprinkled with water of baptism.

An Oration to be said, when the Vesture is put on.

Ancor, Amacor, Amides, Theodonias, Anitor, by the merits of thy Angel, O Lord, I will put on the Garments of Salvation, that this which I desire I may bring to effect: through thee the most holy Adonay, whose kingdom endureth for ever and ever. Amen.

Of the manner of working.

Let the Moon be increasing and equal, if it may then be done, and let her not be combust.

The Operator ought to be clean and purified by the space of nine daies before the beginning of the work, and to be confessed, and receive the holy Communion. Let him have ready the perfume appropriated to the day wherein he would perform the work. He ought also to have holy water from a Priest, and a new earthen vessel with fire, a Vesture and a Pentacle; and let all these things be rightly and duly consecrated and prepared. Let ne of the servants carry the earthen vessel full of fire, and the perfumes, and let another bear the book, another the Garment and Pentacle, and let the master carry the Sword; over which there must be said one mass of the Holy Ghost; and on the middle of the Sword, let there be written this name *Agla* +, and on the other side thereof, this name + On +. And as he goeth to the consecrated place, let him continually read Letanies, the servants answering. And when he cometh to the place where he will ere the Circle, let him draw the lines of the Circle, as we have before taught: and after he hath made it, let him sprinkle the Circle with holy water, saying, *Asperges me Domine, &c.* [Wash me O Lord, &c.]

The Master therefore ought to be purified with fasting, chastity, and abstinency from all luxury the space of three whole dayes before the day of the operation. And on the day that he would do the work, being clothed with pure garments, and furnished with Pentacles, Perfumes, and other things necessary hereunto, let him enter the Circle, and call the Angels from the four parts of the world, which do govern the seven Planets the seven dayes of the week, Colours and Metals; whose name you shall see in their places. And with bended knees invocating the said Angels particularly, let him say, *O Angels supradi i, estote adjutores meæ petitioni, & in adjutorium mihi, in meis rebus & petitionibus.*

Then let him call the Angels from the four parts of the world, that ruke the Air the same day wherein he doth the work or experiment. And having implored specially all the Names and Spirits written in the Circle, let him say, *O vos omnes, adjuro atque contestor per sedem Adonay, per Hagios, ò Theos, Ischyros, Athanatos, Paracletos, Alpha & Omega, & per hæc tria nomina secreta, Agla, On, Tetragrammaton, quòd hodie debeatis adimplere quod cupio.*

These things being performed, let him read the Conjuration assigned for the day wherein he maketh the experiments, as we have before spoken; but if they shall be partinacious and refra ory, and will not yield themselves obedient, neither to the Conjuration assigned to the day, nor to the prayers before made, then use the Conjurations and Exorcismes following.

An Exorcisme of the Spirits of the Air.

Nos facti ad imaginem Dei, & ejus facti voluntate, per potentissimum & corroboratum nomen Dei El, forte & admirabile vos exorcizamus (here he shall name the Spirits he would have appear, of what order soever they be) *& imperamus per eum qui dixit, & fact0um est, & per omnia nomina Dei, & per nomen Adonay, El, Elohim, Elohe, Zebaoth, Elion, Escerchie, Jah, Tetragrammaton, Sadai, Dominus Deus, excelsus, exorcizamus vos, atque potenter imperamus, ut appareatis statim nobis hic juxta Circulum in pulchra forma, videlicet humana, & sine deformitate & tortuositate aliqua. Venite vos omnes tales, quia vobis imperamus, per nomen Y & V quod Adam audivit, & locutus est: & per nomen Dei Agla, quod Loth audivit, & factus salvus cum sua familia: & per nomen Joth, quod Jacob audivit ab Angelo secum lu antes, & liberatus est de manu fratris sui Esau: and by the name Anephexeton, quot Aaron audivit, & loquens, & sapiens factus est: & per nomen Zebaoth, quod Moses nominavit, & omnia flumina & paludes de terra Ægypti, versæ fuerunt in sanguinem: & per nomen Ecerchie Oriston, quod Moses nominavit, & omnes flu vis ebullierunt ranas, & ascenderunt in domos Ægyptiorum, omnia destruentes: & per nomen Elion, quod Moses nominavit, & fuit grando talis, qualis non fuit ab initio mundi: & per nomen Adonay, quod Moses nominavit, & fuerunt locusta, & apparuerunt super terram Ægyptiorum, & comederunt quæ residua erant grandint: & per nomen Schemes amathia, quod Joshua vocavit, & remoratus est Sol cursum: & per nomen Alpha & Omega, quod Daniel nominavit, & destruxit Beel, & Draconem interferit: & in nomine Emmanuel, quod tres pueri, Sidrach, Misach & Abednago, in camino ignis ardentis, cantaverunt, & liberati fuerunt: & per nomen Hagios, & sedem Adonay, & per ò Theos, Iscytos, Athanatos, Paracletus; & per hæc tria secreta nomina, Agla, On, Tetragrammaton, adjuro, contestor, & per hæc nomina, & per alia nomina Domini nostri Dei Omnipotentis, vivi & veri, vos qui vestra culpa de Coelis ejecti fuistis usque ad infernum locum, exorcizamus, & viriliter imperamus, per eum qui dixit, & fa um est, cui omnes obediunt creaturæ, & per illud tremendum Dei judicium: & per mare omnibus incertum, vitreum, quod est amte conspe um divinæ majestatis gradiens, & potestiale: & per quatuor divina animalia T. aniè sedem divinæ majesta is gradientia, & oculos antè & retrò habentia: & per ignem ante ejus thronum circumstantem: & per san os Angelos Cælorum, T. & per eam quæ Ecclesia Dei* *nominatur: & per summam sapientiam Omnipotentis Dei viriliter exorcizamus, ut nobis hic ante Circulum appareatis, ut faciendam nostram voluntatem, in omnibus prout placuerit nobis: per sedem Baldachiæ, & per hoc nomen Primeumaton, quod Moses nominavit, & in cavernis abyssi fuerunt profundati vel absorpti, Datan, Corah & Abiron: & in virtute istius nominis Primeumaton, tota Coeli militia compellente, maledicimus vos, privamus vos omni officio, loco & gaudio vestro, esque in profundum abyssi, & usque ad ultimum diem judicii vos ponimus, & relegamus in ignem æternum, & in stagnum ignis & sulphuris, nisi statim appareatis hic coram nobis, inte Circulum, ad faciendum voluntatem nostram. In omnibus venite per hæc nomina, Adonay Zebaoth, Adonay, Amioram. Venite, venite, imperat vobis Adonay, Saday, Rex regum potentissimus & tremendissimus, cujus vires nulla subterfugere potest creatura vobis pertinacissimis futuris nisi obedieritis, & appareatis ante hunc Circulum, affabiles subito, tandem ruina flebilis miserabilisque, & ignis perpetuum inextinguibilis vos manet. Venite ergo in nomine Adonay Zebaoth, Adonay Amioram: venite, venite, quid tardatis? festinate imperat vobis Adonay, Saday, Rex regum, El, Aty, Titeip, Azia, Hyn, Jen, Minosel, Achadan: Vay, Vaa, Ey, Haa, Eye, Exe, à, El, El, El, à, Hy, Hau, Hau, Hau, Va, Va, Va, Va.*

A Prayer to God, to be said in the four parts of the world, in the Circle.

A Morule, Taneha, Latisten, Rabur, Taneha, Latisten. Escha, Aladia, Alpha & Omega, Leyste, Oriston, Adonay: O my most merciful heavenly Father, have mercy upon me, although a sinner; make appear the arm of thy power in me this day (although thy unworthy child) against these obstinate and pernicious Spirits, that I by thy will may be made a contemplator of thy divine works, and may be illustrated with all wisdom, and alwaies worship and glorifie thy name. I humbly implore and beseech thee, that these Spirits which I call by thy judgement, may be bound and constrained to come, and give true and perfect answers to those things which I shall ask them, and that they may declare and shew unto us those things which by me or s shall be commanded them, not hurting any creature, neither injuring nor terrifying me or my fellows, nor hurting any other creature, and affrighting no man; but let them be obedient to my requests, in all these things which I command them. Then let him stand in the middle of the Circle, and hold his hand towards the Pentacle, and say, *Per Pentaculum Salomonis advocavi, dent mihi responsum verum.*

Then let him say, *Beralanensis, Baldachiensis, Paumachiæ & Apologiæ sedes, per Reges potestaiesiá magnanimas, ac principes præpotentes, genio Liachidæ, ministri tartareæ sedes: Primac, hic princeps sedis Apologiæ nona cohorte: Ego vos invoco, & invocando vos conjure, atque supernæ Majestatis munitus virtute, potenter impero, per eum qui dixit, & fa um est, & cui obediunt omnes creaturæ: & per hoc nomen ineffabile, Tetragrammaton יהוה Jehovah, in quo est plasmatum omne seculum, quo audito elementa corruunt, aër concutitur, mare retrograditur, ignis extinguitur, tera tremit, omnesque exercitus Coelestium, Terrestrium, & Infernorum tremunt, turbantur & corruunt: quatenus citò & sine mora & omni occasione remota, ab universis mundi partibus veniatis, & rationabiliter de omnibus quæcunque interrogavero, respondeatis vos, & veniatis pacifice, visibiles, & affabiles: nunc & sine mora manifestantes quod cupimus: conjurati per nomen æterni vivi & veri Dei Helioren, & mandata nostra per ficientes, persistentes semper usque ad finem, & intentionem meam, visibiles nobis, & affabiles, clara voce nobis, intelligibile, & sine omni ambiguitate.*

Visions and Apparitions.

Quibus ritè peractis is, apparebunt infinitæ visiones, & phantasmata pulsantia organa & omnis generis instrumenta musica, idque sit à spiritibus, ut terrore compulsi socii abeant à Circulo, quia nihil adversus migistrum possunt. Post hæc videbis infinitos sagittarios cum infinita multitudine bestiarum horribilem: quæ ita se componunt, ac si vellent devorare socios: & tamen nil timeant. Tunc Sacerdos sive Magister, adhibent manum Pentaculo, dicat: Fugiat hinc iniquitas vestra, virtute vexilli Dei.

Et tunc Spiritus obedire migistro coguntur, & socii nil amilius videbunt.

Then let the Exorcist say, stretching out his hand to the Pentacle, *Ecce Pentaculum Salomonis, quod ante vestram adduxi præsentiam: ecce personam exorcizatoris on medio Exorcismi, qui est optimà à Deo munitus, intrepidus, providus, qui viribus potens vos exorcizando invocavit & vocat. Venite ergo cum festinotione in virtute nominum istorum, Aye, Saraye, Aye, Saraye, Aye Saraye, ne differatis venire, per nomina æterna Dei vivi & veri Eloy, Archima, Rabur: & per hoc præsens Pentaculum, quod super vos potenter imperat: & per virutem coelestium Spirituum dominorum vestrorum: & per personam exorcizatoris, conjurati, festinati venire & obedire præceptori vestro, qui vocatur O inomos. Hisperactis, sibiles in quatuor angulis mundi. Et videbis immediate magnos motus: & cum videris, dicas: Quid tardatis? Quid moramini? quid fa is? præparate vos & obedite præceptori vesto, in nomine Domini Bathat, vel Vachat super Abrac ruens, super veniens, Abeor super Aberer.*

Tunc immediatè venient in sua forma propria. Et quando videbis eos juxta Circulum, ostende illis Pentaculum coopertum syndone sacro, & discooperiatur, & dicat: Ecce conclusionem vestram, nolite fieri inobedientes. Et subito videbis eos in pacifica forma: & dicent tibi, Pete quid vis, quia nos sumus parati complere omnia mandata tua, quia dominus ad hæc nos subjugavit. Cum autem apparuerint Spiritus, tunc dicas, Bene veneritis Spiritus, vel reges nobilissimi, quia vos vocavi per illum cui omne genufle itur, coelestium, terrestrium & infernorum: cujus in manu omnia regna regum sunt, nec est qui suæ contrarius esse possit Majestati. Quatenus constringo vos, ut hic ante circulum visibes, affabiles permanetis, tamdiu tamque constantes, nec sint licentia mea recedatis, donec meam sine fallacia aliqua & veredicè perficiatis voluntatem, per potentiæ illius virtutem, qui mare posuit terminum suum, quem præterire non potest, & lege illius potentiæ, non periransit fines suos, Dei scilicet altissimi, regis, domini, qui cun a creavit, Amen.

Then command what you will, and it shall be done. Afterwards license them thus: + *In nomine Patris, + Filii, & + Spiritus sacti, ite in pace ad loca vestra: & pax sit inter nos & vos, parati sitis venire vocati.*

These are the things which *Peter de Abano* hath spoken concerning Magical Elements.

But that you may the better know the manner of composing a Circle, I will set down one Scheme; so that if any one would make a Circle in Spring-time for the first hour of Lords day, it must be in the same manner as is the figure following.

The figure of a Circle for the first hour of the Lords day, in Spring-time.

It remaineth now, That we explain the week, the several dayes thereof: and first of the Lords day.

Considerations of the Lords day

The Angel of the Lords day, his Sigil, Planet, the Signe of
the Planet, and the name of the fourth heaven.

THE ANGELS OF THE LORDS DAY.

Michael.   *Dardiel.*   *Huratapal.*

THE ANGELS OF THE AIR RULING ON THE LORDS DAY.

Varcan.   *King.*

HIS MINISTERS.

Tus.   *Andas.*   *Cynabal*

THE WINDE WHICH THE ANGELS OF THE ABOVESAID ARE UNDER.

The North-Winde

Of the Names of the Hours, and the Angels ruling them.

THE ANGEL OF THE FOURTH HEAVEN, RULING ON THE LORDS DAY, WHICH OUGHT TO BE CALED FROM THE FOUR PARTS OF THE WORLD.

TO THE EAST.

Samael. *Baciel.* *Atel.* *Gabriel.* *Vionairaba.*

TO THE WEST.

Anael. *Pabel.* *Ustael.* *Burchat.* *Suceratos.* *Capabili.*

TO THE NORTH.

Aiel. *Aniel.* *Vel Aquiel.* *Masgabriel.* *Sapiel.* *Matuyel.*

TO THE SOUTH.

Haludiel. *Machasiel.* *Charsiel.* *Uriel.* *Noramiel.*

THE PERFUME OF THE LORDS DAY.

Red Wheat.

The Conjuration of the Lords day.

Conjuro & confirmo super vos Angeli fortes Dei, & sancti, in nomine Adonay, Eye, Eye, Eye, qui est ille, qui fuit, est & erit, Eye, Abraye: & in nomine Saday, Cados, Cados, Cados, alie sendentis super Cherubin, & per nomen magnum ipsius Dei fortis & potentis, exaltatique super omnes coelos, Eye, Saraye, plasmatoris seculorum, qui creavit mundum, coelum, terram, mare, & omnia quæ in eis sunt in primo die, & sigillavit ea san o nomine suo Phaa: & per nomina sanorum Angelorum, qui dominantur in quarto exercitu, & serviunt coram potentissimo Salamia, Angelo magno & honorato: & per nomen stellæ, quæ est Sol, & per signum, & per immensum nomen Dei vivi, & per nomina omnia prædi a, conjuro te Michael angele magne, qui es præpositus Diei Dominicæ: & per nomen Adona, Dei Israel, qui creavit mundum & quicquid in eo est, quod pro melabores, & ad moleas omnem meam petitionem, juxta meum velle & votum meum, in negotio & causa mea. And here thou shalt declare thy cause and business, and for what thing thou makest this Conjuration.

The Spirits of the Air of the Lords day, are under the North-winde; their nature is to procure Gold, Gemmes, Carbuncles, Riches; to cause one to obtain favour and benevolence; to dissolve the enmities of men; to raise men to honors; to carry or take away infirmities. But in what manner they appear, it's spoken already in the former book of Magical Ceremonies.

Of the Names of the Hours, and the Angels ruling them.

Considerations of munday.

The Angel of Munday, his Sigil, Planet, the Signe of the Planet, and name of the first heaven.

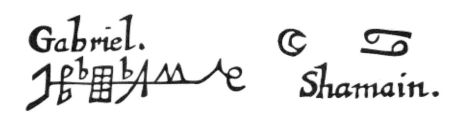

THE ANGELS OF MUNDAY.

Gabriel.   *Michael.*   *Samael.*

THE ANGELS OF THE AIR RULING MUNDAY.

Arcan.   *King.*

HIS MINISTERS.

Bilet.   *Missabu.*   *Abuzaba.*

THE WINDE WHICH THE SAID ANGELS OF THE AIR ARE SUBJECT TO.

The West-winde.

THE ANGELS OF THE FIRST HEAVEN, RULING ON MUNDAY, WHICH OUGHT TO BE CALLED FROM THE FOUR PARTS OF THE WORLD.

FROM THE EAST.

Gabriel.   *Gabrael.*   *Madiel.*   *Deamiel.*   *Janael.*

FROM THE WEST.

Sachiel.   *Zaniel.*   *Habaiel.*   *Bachanael.*   *Corabael.*

FROM THE NORTH.

Mael.   *Vuael.*   *Valnum.*   *Baliel.*   *Balay.*   *Humastrau.*

FROM THE SOUTH.

Curaniel.   *Dabriel.*   *Darquiel.*   *Hanun.*   *Anayl.*   *Vetuel.*

THE PERFUME OF MUNDAY.

Aloes.

Of the Names of the Hours, and the Angels ruling them.

The Conjuration of Munday.

The Angel of Tuesday, his Sigil, Planet, the Signe of the Planet, and name of the first heaven.

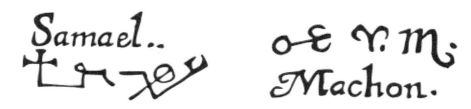

THE ANGELS OF TUESDAY.

Samael.   *Satael.*   *Amabiel*

THE ANGELS OF THE AIR RULING TUESDAY.

Samax.   *King.*

HIS MINISTERS.

Carmax.   *Ismoli.*   *Paffram.*

THE WINDE WHICH THE SAID ANGELS OF THE AIR ARE SUBJECT TO.

The East-winde.

THE ANGELS OF THE FIRST HEAVEN, RULING ON TUESDAY, WHICH OUGHT TO BE CALLED FROM THE FOUR PARTS OF THE WORLD.

FROM THE EAST.

Friagne.   *Guael.*   *Damael.*   *Calzas.*   *Arragon.*

FROM THE WEST.

Lama.   *Astagna.*   *Lobquin.*   *Soncas.*   *Jazel.*   *Isiael.*   *Irel.*

FROM THE NORTH.

Rahumel.   *Hyniel.*   *Rayel.*   *Seraphiel.*   *Matheil.*   *Fraciel.*

FROM THE SOUTH.

Sacriel.   *Janiel.*   *Galdel.*   *Osael.*   *Vianuel.*   *Zaliel.*

THE PERFUME OF TUESDAY.

Pepper.

The Conjuration of Tuesday.

Conjuro & confirmo super vos, Angeli fortes & sacti, per nomen Ya, Ya, Ya, He, He, He, Va, Hy, Hy, Ha, Ha, Ha, Va, Va, Va, An, An, An, Aie, Aie, Aie, El, Ay, Elibra, Eloim, Eloim: & per nomina ipsius alti Dei, qui secit aquam aridam apparere, & vocavit terram, & produxit arbores, & herbas de ea, & sigillavit super eam cum precioso, honorato, metuendo & sancto nomine suo: & per nomen angelorum dominantium in quinto exercitu, qui serviunt Acimoy Angelo magno, forti, potenti, & honorato: & per nomen Stellæ, quæ est Mars: & per nomina prædicta conjuro super te Samael, Angele magne, qui præpositus es diei Martis: & per nomina Adonay, Dei vivi & veri, quod pro me labores, & adimpleas, &c. As in the Conjuration of Sunday.

The Spirits of the Air of Tuesday are under the East-winde: their nature is to cause wars, mortality, death and combustions; and to give two thousand Souldiers at a time; to bring death, infirmities or health. The manner of their appearing you may see in the former book.

Considerations of Wednesday.

The Angel of Wednesday, his Sigil, Planet, the Signe of the Planet, and name of the first heaven.

THE ANGELS OF WEDNESDAY.

Raphael.   *Miel.*   *Seraphiel*

THE ANGELS OF THE AIR RULING WEDNESDAY.

Mediat, or Modiat..   *King.*

HIS MINISTERS.

Suquinos.   *Sallases.*

THE WINDE WHICH THE SAID ANGELS OF THE AIR ARE SUBJECT TO.

The Southwest-winde.

THE ANGELS OF THE FIRST HEAVEN, RULING ON WEDNESDAY, WHICH OUGHT TO BE CALLED FROM THE FOUR PARTS OF THE WORLD.

FROM THE EAST.

Mathlai.   *Tarmiel.*   *Baraborat.*

FROM THE WEST.

Jeresous.   *Mitraton.*

FROM THE NORTH.

Theil. *Rael.* *Jariahel.* *Venahel.* *Velel.* *Abuiori.* *Ucirnuel.*

FROM THE SOUTH.

Milliel. *Nelapa.* *Babel.* *Caluel.* *Vel.* *Laquel.*

THE PERFUME OF WEDNESDAY.

Mastick.

The Conjuration of Wednesday.

Conjuro & confirmo vos angeli fortes, sancti & potentes, in nomine fortis, metuendissimi & benedicti Ja, Adonay, Eloim, Saday, Saday, Saday, Eie, Eie, Eie, Asamie, Asaraie: & in nomine Adonay Dei Israel, qui creavit luminaria magna, ad distinguendum diem à nocte: & per nomen omnium Angelorum deservientium in exercitu secundo coram Tetra Angelo majori, atque forti & potenti: & per nomen Stellæ, quæ est Mercurius: & per nomen Sigilli, quæ sigillatur a Deo fortissimo & honoratio: per omnia prædi a super te Raphael Angele magne, conjuro, qui es præpositus die: quartæ: & per nomen san um quod erat scriptum in fronte Aaron sacerdotis altissimi creatoris: & per nomina Angelorum qui in gratiam Salvatoris confirmati sunt: & per nomen sedis Animalium, habentium senas alas, quòd pro me labo, et, &c. As in the Conjuration of Sunday.

The Spirits of the Air of Wednesday are subje to the South-west-winde: their nature is to give all Metals; to reveal all earthly things past, present and to come; to pacifie judges, to give victories in war, to re-edifie, and teach experiments and all decayed Sciences, and to change bodies mixt of Elements conditionally out of one into another; to give infirmities or health; to raise the poor, and cast down the high ones; to binde or lose Spirits; to open locks or bolts: such-kinde of Spirits have the operation of others, but not in their perfect power, but in virtue or knowledge. The what manner they appear, it is before spoken.

Of the Names of the Hours, and the Angels ruling them.

Considerations of Thursday.

The Angel of Thursday, his Sigil, Planet, the Signe of the Planet, and name of the first heaven.

THE ANGELS OF THURSDAY.

Sachiel. *Castiel.* *Asasiel*

THE ANGELS OF THE AIR RULING THURSDAY.

Suth. King.

HIS MINISTERS.

Maguth. *Gutrix.*

THE WINDE WHICH THE SAID ANGELS OF THE AIR ARE SUBJECT TO.

The South-winde.

THE ANGELS OF THE FIRST HEAVEN, RULING ON THURSDAY, WHICH OUGHT TO BE CALLED FROM THE FOUR PARTS OF THE WORLD.

FROM THE EAST.

O Deus, magne & excelse, & honorate, per infinita secula.

FROM THE WEST.

O Deus sapiens, & clare, & juste, ac divina clementia: ego rogo te piissime Pater, quòd meam petitionem, quòd meum opus, & meum laborem hodie debeam complere, & perfe è intelligere. Tu qui vivis & regnas per infinita secula seculorum, Amen.

FROM THE NORTH.

O Deus potens, fortis, & sine principio.

FROM THE SOUTH.

O Deus potens & Misericors.

THE PERFUME OF THURSDAY.

Saffron.

The Conjuration of Thursday.

Conjuro & confirmo super vos, Angeli sancti, per nomen, Cados, Cados, Cados, Eschereie, Eschereie, Eschereie, Hatim ya, fortis firmator seculorum, Cantine, Jaym, Janic, Anic, Calbat, Sabbac, Berifay, Alnaym: & per nomen Adonay, qui creavit pisces reptilia in aquis, & aves super faciem terræ, volantes versus coelos die quinto: & per nomina Angelorum serventium in sexto exercitu coram pastore Angelo san o & magno & potenti principe: & per nomen stellæ, quæ est Jupiter: & per nomen Sigilli sui: & per nomen Adonay, summi Dei, omnium creatoris: & per nomen omnium stellarum, & per vim & virtutem earum: & per nomina prædi a, conjuro te Sachiel Angele magne, qui es præpositus dici Jovis, ut pro me labores, &c. As in the Conjuration of the Lords day.

The Spirits of the Air of Thursday, are subje to the South-winde; their nature is to procure the love of woman; to cause men to be merry and joyful; to pacifie strife and contentions; to appease enemies; to heal the diseased, and to disease the whole; and procureth losses, or taketh them away. Their manner of appearing is spoken of already.

Considerations of Friday.

The Angel of Friday, his Sigil, Planet, the Signe of the Planet, and name of the first heaven.

THE ANGELS OF FRIDAY.

Anael.   *Racheil.*   *Sachiel.*

THE ANGELS OF THE AIR RULING FRIDAY.

Sarabotes.   King.

HIS MINISTERS.

Amabiel.   *Aba.*   *Abalidoth.*   *Flaef.*

THE WINDE WHICH THE SAID ANGELS OF THE AIR ARE SUBJECT TO.

The West-winde.

THE ANGELS OF THE FIRST HEAVEN, RULING ON FRIDAY, WHICH OUGHT TO BE CALLED FROM THE FOUR PARTS OF THE WORLD.

FROM THE EAST.

Setchiel.   *Chedusitaniel.*   *Corat.*   *Tamael.*   *Tenaciel.*

FROM THE WEST.

Turiel.   *Coniel.*   *Babiel.*   *Kadie.*   *Maltiel.*   *Huphatiel.*

FROM THE NORTH.

Peniel.   *Pemael.*   *Penat.*   *Raphael.*   *Raniel.*   *Doremiel.*

FROM THE SOUTH.

Porna.   *Sachiel.*   *Chermiel.*   *Samael.*   *Santanael.*   *Famiel.*

THE PERFUME OF FRIDAY.

Pepperwort.

The Conjuration of Friday.

Conjuro & confirmo super vos Angeli fortes, sancti atque potentes, in nomine On, Hey, Heya, Ja, Je, Adonay, Saday, & in nomine Saday, qui creavit quadrupedia & anamalia reptilia, & homines in sexto die, & Adæ dedit potestatem super omnia animalia: unde benedi um sit nomen creatoris in loco suo: & per nomina Angelorum servientium in tertio exercitu, coram Dagiel Angelo magno, principe forti atque potenti: & per nomen Stellæ quæ est Venus: & per Sigillum ejus, quod quidem est san um: & per nomina prædi a conjuro super te Anael, qui es præpositus diei sextæ, ut pro me labores, &c. As before in the Conjuration of Sunday.

The Spirits of the Air of Friday are subject to the West-winde; their nature is to give silver: to excite men, and incline them to luxury; to reconcile enemies through luxury; and o make marriages; to allure men to love women; to cause, or take away infirmities; and to do all things which have motion.

Of the Names of the Hours, and the Angels ruling them.

Considerations of Saturday, or the Sabbath day.

The Angel of Saturday, his Sigil, Planet, the Signe of the Planet, and name of the first heaven.

THE ANGELS OF SATURDAY.

Cassiel.   *Machatan.*   *Uriel.*

THE ANGELS OF THE AIR RULING SATURDAY.

Maymon.   King.

HIS MINISTERS.

Abumalith.   *Assaibi.*   *Balidet.*

THE WINDE WHICH THE SAID ANGELS OF THE AIR ARE SUBJECT TO.

The Southwest-winde.

THE PERFUME OF SATURDAY.

Pepperwort.

The Conjuration of Saturday.

Conjuro & confirmo super vos Caphriel vel Cassiel, Machatori, & Seraquiel Angeli fortes & potentes: & per nomen Adonay, Adonay, Adonay, Eie, Eie, Eie, Acim, Acim, Acin, Cados, Cados, Ina vel Ima, Ima, Saclay, Ja, Sar, Domini formatoris seculorum, qui in septimo die quie vt: & per illum qui in beneplacito suo filiis Israel in hereditatem observandum dedit, ut eum firmiter custodirent, & san ificarent, ad habendem inde bonam in alio seculo remunerationem: & per nomina Angelorum servientium in exercitu septimo Pooel Angelo magno & potenti principi: & per nomen stellæ quæ est Saturnus: & per san um Sigillum ejus: & per nomina prædi a conjuro super te Caphriel, qui præpositus es diei septimæ, quæ est dies Sabbati, quòd pro me labores, &c. As is set down in the Conjuration of the Lords day.

The Spirits of the Air of Saturday are subje to the Southwest- inde: the nature of them is to sow discordes, hatred, evil thoughts and cogitations; to give leave freely, to slay and kill every one, and to lame or maim every member. Their manner of appearing is declared in the former book.

31

Of the Names of the Hours, and the Angels ruling them.

Tables of the Angels of the Hours, according to the course of the dayes.

SUNDAY

Hours of the day.	Angels of the hours.	Hours of the day.	Angels of the hours.
1. Yayn.	Michael.	7. Ourer.	Samael.
2. Janor	Anael.	8. Tanic.	Michael.
3. Nasnia.	Raphael.	9. Neron.	Anael.
4, Salla.	Gabriel.	10. Jayon.	Raphael.
5. Sadedali.	Cassiel.	11. Abay.	Gabriel.
6. Thamur.	Sachiel.	12. Natalon.	Cassiel.

SUNDAY NIGHT

Hours of the day.	Angels of the hours.	Hours of the day.	Angels of the hours.
1. Beron	Sachiel.	7. Netos.	Cassiel.
2. Barol.	Samael.	8. Tafrae.	Sachiel.
3. Thanu.	Michael.	9. Saffur.	Samael.
4. Athir.	Anael.	10. Aglo.	Michael..
5. Mathun.	Raphael.	11. Calerna.	Anael.
6. Rana.	Gabriel.	12. Salam.	Raphael.

MUNDAY

Hours of the day.	Angels of the hours.	Hours of the night.	Angels of the hours.
1. Yayn.	Gabriel.	1. Beron.	Anael.
2. Janor.	Cassiel.	2. Barol.	Raphael.
3. Nasnia.	Sachiel.	3. Thanu.	Gabriel.
4. Salla.	Samael.	4. Athir.	Cassiel.
5. Sadedali.	Michael.	5. Mathon.	Sacheil.
6. Thamur.	Anael.	6. Rana.	Samael.
7. Ourer.	Raphael.	7. Netos.	Michael.
8. Tanic.	Gabriel.	8. Tafrae.	Anael.
9. Neron.	Cassiel.	9. Sassur.	Raphael.
10. Jayon.	Sachiel.	10. Aglo.	Gabriel.
11. Abay,.	Samael.	11. Calerna.	Cassiel.
12. Natalon.	Michael.	12. Salam.	Sacheil.

Of the Names of the Hours, and the Angels ruling them.

TUESDAY

Hours of the day.	Angels of the hours.	Hours of the night.	Angels of the hours.
1. Yayn.	Samael.	1. Beron.	Cassiel.
2. Janor.	Michael.	2. Barol.	Sachiel.
3. Nasnia.	Anael.	3. Thanu.	Samael.
4. Salla.	Raphael.	4. Athir.	Michael.
5. Sadedali.	Gabriel.	5. Mathon.	Anael.
6. Thamur	Cassiel.	6. Rana.	Raphael.
7. Ourer.	Sachiel.	7. Netos.	Gabriel.
8. Tanic.	Samael.	8. Tafrae.	Cassiel.
9. Neron	Michael.	9. Sassur.	Sachiel.
10. Jayon.	Anael.	10. Aglo.	Samael.
11. Abay	Raphael.	11. Calerna.	Michael.
12. Natalon.	Gabriel.	12. Salam.	Anael.

WEDNESDAY

Hours of the day.	Angels of the hours.	Hours of the night.	Angels of the hours.
1. Yayn.	Raphael.	1. Yayn.	Michael.
2. Janor.	Gabriel.	2. Janor.	Anael.
3. Nasnia.	Cassiel.	3. Nasnia.	Raphael.
4. Salla.	Sachiel.	4. Salla.	Gabriel.
5. Sadedali.	Samael.	5. Sadedali.	Cassiel.
6. Thamur	Michael.	6. Thamur	Sachiel.
7. Ourer.	Anael.	7. Ourer.	Samael.
8. Tanic.	Raphael.	8. Tanic.	Michael.
9. Neron	Gabriel.	9. Neron	Anael.
10. Jayon.	Cassiel.	10. Jayon.	Raphael.
11. Abay	Sachiel.	11. Abay	Gabriel.
12. Natalon.	Samael.	12. Natalon.	Cassiel.

THURSDAY

Hours of the day.	Angels of the hours.	Hours of the night.	Angels of the hours.
1. Yayn.	Sachiel.	1. Yayn.	Gabriel.
2. Janor.	Samael.	2. Janor.	Cassiel.
3. Nasnia.	Michael.	3. Nasnia.	Sachiel.
4. Salla.	Anael.	4. Salla.	Samael.
5. Sadedali.	Raphael.	5. Sadedali.	Michael.
6. Thamur	Gabriel.	6. Thamur	Anael.
7. Ourer.	Cassiel.	7. Ourer.	Raphael.
8. Tanic.	Sachiel.	8. Tanic.	Gabriel.
9. Neron	Samael.	9. Neron	Cassiel.
10. Jayon.	Michael.	10. Jayon.	Sachiel.
11. Abay	Anael.	11. Abay	Samael.
12. Natalon.	Raphael.	12. Natalon.	Michael.

Heptameron: or, Magical Elements of Peter de Abano, philosopher

FRIDAY

Hours of the day.	Angels of the hours.	Hours of the night.	Angels of the hours.
1. Yayn.	Anael.	1. Yayn.	Samael.
2. Janor.	Raphael.	2. Janor.	Michael.
3. Nasnia.	Gabriel.	3. Nasnia.	Anael.
4. Salla.	Cassiel.	4. Salla.	Raphael.
5. Sadedali.	Sachiel.	5. Sadedali.	Gabriel.
6. Thamur	Samael.	6. Thamur	Cassiel.
7. Ourer.	Michael.	7. Ourer.	Sachiel.
8. Tanic.	Anael.	8. Tanic.	Samael.
9. Neron	Raphael.	9. Neron	Michael.
10. Jayon.	Gabriel.	10. Jayon.	Anael.
11. Abay	Cassiel.	11. Abay	Raphael.
12. Natalon.	Sachiel.	12. Natalon.	Gabriel.

Of the Names of the Hours, and the Angels ruling them.

SATURDAY

Hours of the day.	Angels of the hours.	Hours of the night.	Angels of the hours.
1. Yayn.	Cassiel.	1. Yayn.	Raphael.
2. Janor.	Sachiel.	2. Janor.	Gabriel.
3. Nasnia.	Samael.	3. Nasnia.	Cassiel.
4. Salla.	Michael.	4. Salla.	Sachiel.
5. Sadedali.	Anael.	5. Sadedali.	Samael.
6. Thamur	Raphael.	6. Thamur	Michael.
7. Ourer.	Gabriel.	7. Ourer.	Anael.
8. Tanic.	Cassiel.	8. Tanic.	Raphael.
9. Neron	Sachiel.	9. Neron	Gabriel.
10. Jayon.	Samael.	10. Jayon.	Cassiel.
11. Abay	Michael.	11. Abay	Sachiel.
12. Natalon.	Anael.	12. Natalon.	Samael.

37

But this is to be observed by the way, that the first hour of the day, of every Country, and in every season whatsoever, is to be assigned to the Sun-rising, when he first appeareth arising in the horizon: and the first hour of the night is to be the thirteenth hour, from the first hour of the day. But of these things it is sufficiently spoken.

FINIS.

Alphabetical Index

Heptameron: or, Magical Elements of Peter de Abano, philosopher

Of the Names of the Hours, and the Angels ruling them.

Of the Names of the Hours, and the Angels ruling them.

43

Heptameron: or, Magical Elements of Peter de Abano, philosopher

Printed in Great Britain
by Amazon

45791721R00031